Shadowlands to the Songs of Seraphim

Also by Erik V. Sahakian

Check Yourself Before You Wreck Yourself
Where to Put the Ladder (co-author)
Don't Worry About A Thing
Follow Me
Out of the Shadowlands

Shadowlands to the Songs of Seraphim

A Poetic Testimony of a Life Transformed by Jesus

Erik V. Sahakian

Shadowlands to the Songs of Seraphim
Copyright © 2013 by Erik V. Sahakian

ALL RIGHTS RESERVED
No portion of this book may be reproduced, stored in any retrieval system, or transmitted in any form or by any means, electronic, mechanical, photocopy, recording or otherwise, without the express written consent of the author.

Cover Design/Layout: Andrew Enos
Cover Photograph: Marko Horvat

All Scripture is taken from the New King James Version of the Bible. Copyright © 1979, 1980, 1982 by Thomas Nelson, Inc. Used by permission. All rights reserved.

Library of Congress Control Number: 2011934398

ISBN 978-0-9852857-0-8
Second Printing: December 2017

FOR INFORMATION CONTACT:

Wildwood Ignited Publishing:
A Ministry of Wildwood Calvary Chapel
35145 Oak Glen Rd
Yucaipa, CA 92399
www.wildwoodcalvarychapel.com

www.eriksahakian.com

Printed in the United States of America

This book is dedicated to my wife Juanita, and my children Skylar and Maksim, who have all given me the best memories and joys of my life.

Contents

Acknowledgements / 9

Foreword / 11

Preface / 15

Silent Euphoria / 19

Cherish These Dreams / 25

Idyllwild / 29

Sweet Night / 33

Shadowlands / 37

Company of Wolves / 43

Innocent Surrender / 47

The Canopy of Leaves / 51

Suspended in Autumn / 55

Heavenly Father / 59

The Secluded Meadow / 63

April / 67

The Night Terror / 71

Skylar's Lullaby / 77

Sereja / 81

A Friend's Sonnet / 89

The Dreamer / 95

Life Without You / 99

The Dying Prayer of General Armistead / 103

A Child's Prayer / 109

Ending with the Beginning / 113

Final Thoughts / 117

A Prayer of Repentance and Salvation / 123

Moving Forward / 125

Acknowledgements

Juanita, my wife, I love you more than words can express. Thank you for being supportive and always making me laugh. Your consistent willingness to submit to the leading of the Holy Spirit in our lives is an inspiration to me. You are my best friend.

Skylar and Maksim, it is my complete honor and joy that God chose me to be your father. I am so proud of you both. I can't wait to see the impact you will make on the world around you for Jesus Christ. Every day I look forward to waking up in the morning to share another special day with you guys. Thank you for filling my life with laughter.

I want to give a special thanks to my father, Ernest Sahakian, who taught me what it truly means to be a godly man. You are my hero and I thank God for blessing me with an example like you.

I am blessed by the contributions that Pastor Scott Wright made to this book by reminding me that every opportunity to share our lives is an opportunity to share the gospel, and in doing so, an opportunity to reach the lost and challenge the saved. Scott is a gifted teacher, biblical expositor, and a good friend.

Foreword

Have you ever looked back on your life and wondered how different it would be if you had made different choices? Have you wondered where God was when you needed Him most? Have you found yourself depressed, discouraged, or just plain lacking hope at various times throughout your life? Have you not forgiven yourself for something in your past—something you did or didn't do? We are told in Romans 8:28 that "all things work together for good to those who love God, to those who are the called according to His purpose."

Shadowlands to the Songs of Seraphim is an amazing collection of poems spanning over twenty years of Erik Sahakian's life. What makes this collection so unique is that almost two decades after the original poem was penned, Erik was prompted by the Holy Spirit to write a corresponding message for each poem, explaining what was going on in his life at the time of the original writing. Through each of these messages, you are invited to journey through the eyes, mind, and heart of this Christian man and experience what he was facing, feeling, and even fearing, as he put his pen to paper.

These poems are so amazingly unique and perfectly explained in detail; it is easy to see the sovereignty of God's perfect plan working in and throughout Erik's life. It's almost as if each of these poems make up their own squiggly line and as you gather them all together in one collection, you can clearly see the individual lines now making the image of a complete fingerprint of God on Erik's life.

As you read this book, you will find yourself reflecting on your own personal experiences which you have encountered on the path throughout your life's journey. You, too, will quickly be able to identify and acknowledge how God has been with you from the very beginning. Know this—if you are willing to be used for the purpose in which He has created you, then you will soon realize God has a perfect plan for using every one of those experiences for good in your life too.

I want to encourage you to prayerfully read this book and allow God to reveal everything He wishes to you. Be willing to allow God to show you where He has guided you in the past and where He wants to guide you today, as well as tomorrow. I pray this book impacts you as it has impacted my life.

Scott F. Wright
Pastor and founder of *mydailydose.org*

Blessed is the man who walks not in the counsel of the ungodly, nor stands in the path of sinners, nor sits in the seat of the scornful; but his delight is in the law of the Lord, and in His law he meditates day and night. He shall be like a tree planted by the rivers of water, that brings forth its fruit in its season, whose leaf shall not wither; and whatever he does shall prosper.

Psalm 1:1-3

Preface

I wrote my first poem when I was sitting in my sophomore English class, lamenting the loss of a close friend who had changed for the worse since dating one of the popular guys on campus. It happened seemingly by accident. I wasn't paying particularly close attention to the topic the teacher was lecturing about because my heart was very heavy regarding my friend who appeared to have abandoned everything she had once stood for, simply to be popular. I sensed in my heart there was a profound spiritual truth in the circumstances surrounding these events and all I remember is picking up my pen and writing down my thoughts. I was actually surprised how easily the words flowed onto the paper. Strangely, the opportunity to express these emotions helped me to make sense of the whole situation. From then on, I would often find myself expressing my heart through writing.

The freedom of expressing thoughts and emotions through writing wasn't a totally undiscovered idea to me. I had been writing movie scripts since I was in elementary school. I imagined myself to be the next Steven Spielberg, so I took these stories very seriously. I'm embarrassed to admit I even ended a childhood friendship once because I thought a buddy of mine had stolen one of my movie ideas! In these stories I was the bold adventurer that I was too timid to be in real life, the hero that saved the world or the damsel in distress.

Writing fiction had always been an outlet for my ideas, dreams, beliefs, and feelings. I was painfully shy around other kids, especially in junior high because my classmates made childhood cruelty an exact science. But poetry, which I *thought* I had stumbled on purely by accident, was different. It was a simple way to express my feelings in a few short lines, without having to devise a plot around it. I soon found myself abandoning fictional stories for writings that were inspired by spiritual events in my "real" life. I later realized that there was nothing accidental about my poems because their onset came at the exact same time that I fully gave my heart to Jesus Christ.

The poems I write are not forced. In fact, even to this very day I can't just sit down at a desk and write a poem. Poetry comes to me as suddenly as a storm in the middle of summer. I don't plan on them—they just happen. When the Holy Spirit puts a poem in my heart, nothing can hold it back. Yet, when I strive in the flesh to write something, it normally turns out to be a disaster! I actually prefer it this way because I trust the Holy Spirit, whereas I don't trust myself, and it also keeps me fully aware that God deserves all the glory!

One thing I really enjoy about poetry is that we can read the same poem and yet understand it differently because we all have a natural tendency to decipher information in the context of our own personal experiences. As we grow over time, our understanding grows as well.

At the same time, regardless of the reader's interpretation, the writer did have a specific feeling or idea they were trying to convey, and that exists independent of the reader's understanding. I want everyone who reads this book to experience both aspects of my poetry. I want you to take from it your own interpretation at first, but I also want you to know how God inspired me to write each poem. So following each poem is a scriptural commentary to give you insight into what the Lord was speaking to my heart at the time the poem was written.

This collection of poems that you now hold in your hands spans over two decades of my life and not just any decades, but the most formative ones in which I graduated from high school and college, met and married my wife, became a father, and truly came to joyfully embrace God's calling on my life.

I hope that you enjoy this collection of writings. They are not meant to impress (some I like less than others), but all are simply designed to express lessons I learned at specific points in my walk with Jesus.

So with all that in mind, let's jump right in! I hope you have as much fun reading them as I did writing them.

Silent Euphoria

Sparkling streams of sweetened nectar
Chase the shadows far from me.
In woodland groves of silent secrets
May my dreams run wild and free.

To the heights, beyond the climbs
Into ethereal worlds of light.
As the candles flicker on
Dancing in veils of twilight.

Let Love's rain descend upon
Peace so pure in elegance.
Hence the forests softly sing
Of secrets held in quietness.

Through the wisp of tranquil mist
Dreams become sweet symphonies.
Listening close to ancient song
Nature cries Love's melodies.

Show me love, oh beauty be
Are there dreams more pure than these?
As I gaze betwixt the blades
At creation bowing its knees.

Who is faithful, who is Love?
Only one can claim that throne.

As Love's peace from crimson flow
Reminds the soul of what is known.

So hand in hand to paradise
In gentle meadows gales blow.
In golden rays an eternal embrace
As night begets the dawn of gold.

Peace. That is what inspired this poem. Not only is the imagery and symbolism peaceful, but reading the poem out loud even *sounds* peaceful.

Peace is such a fragile and elusive gift in the eyes of this sinful world. Nations, people, and families often strive and struggle in their vain attempt to have peace apart from God. Even people who reject God say they want an end to war, for diverse groups to come together in unity, for families to get along, and for individuals to have inner peace; yet, the sinful nature of this fallen world will always confound their plans and dash their hopes on the rock of truth. The reality is that *real* peace can only come from God, by living a life that has been made right with God. Any other form of peace is simply a facade or a poor reflection of the real thing and that is why it never lasts.

Paul wrote in Philippians 4:6-7 that we should "Be anxious for nothing, but in everything by prayer and supplication, with thanksgiving, let your requests be made known to God; and the peace of God, which surpasses all understanding, will guard your hearts and minds through Christ Jesus."

Imagine what this world would give for the kind of inner peace that "surpasses all understanding"! Of course, this peace *is* available to all mankind, but only through Jesus Christ, the Prince of Peace (Isaiah 9:6).

Due to sin, all people are automatically born into an estranged relationship with their heavenly Father. This barrier needs to be removed for restoration to take place and that was accomplished by Christ's redemptive work on the cross. Each person must then choose to receive this gift in faith and follow Him. As it says in Romans 5:1, "Therefore, having been justified by faith, we have peace with God through our Lord Jesus Christ."

Peace *with* God brings the peace *of* God and that is the peace that surpasses all understanding. But notice in both Philippians 4:7 and Romans 5:1 that the source of true peace is always Jesus Christ. He is the only way. The world wants peace apart from Christ and, sadly, this is the very reason why they cannot have it.

The peace of God is a tranquility that defies earthly words to explain. I have had numerous times in my life where I literally felt like my entire world was collapsing all around me; yet, I felt no anxiety or worry. I only felt peace because I knew that I was safe in God's arms and He was the one leading my life. That is the very reason this kind of peace surpasses understanding because it isn't a natural peace, it is a supernatural peace, and the world can neither duplicate it nor understand it.

I hope it encourages you to know that in Christ this peace is not an elusive gift but one that is readily available if you would only swallow your pride, ask God for it, and have faith that He will deliver. Notice back to Philippians 4:6 that it was "by prayer and supplication, with thanksgiving" that our requests should be made known to God and the peace of God, through Christ, will follow.

God is not playing a game of cosmic hide-and-seek with us! It makes me think of when my son, Maksim, was a toddler. When I played hide-and-seek with him he always stood in a very obvious place so that I would easily find him. He *wanted* to be found! God is the same way. He wants to be found and He is standing with His arms wide open to you. Won't you have faith in Jesus Christ and the peace that only He can bring?

"Ask, and it will be given to you; seek, and you will find; knock, and it will be opened to you. For everyone who asks receives, and he who seeks finds, and to him who knocks it will be opened."

Matthew 7:7-8

"Now the God of peace be with you all. Amen."

Romans 15:33

Cherish These Dreams

Cherish the Spirit's dreams and make them your own
For they are the wings of your soul.
Like the breezes of spring that bring peace to your heart
Let these dreams caress your soul.

For life is more than what it may seem
It can be a world of wondrous delight!
For only in His dreams are you truly free
To allow your destiny to take flight.

So ride the wind into the night
Where young children softly play.
And cherish these dreams as a gift from God
For each dream brings a new dawn of day.

My heart breaks whenever I look at the world around me and I see lost people, whose lives were created with so much purpose and meaning, being deceived into squandering their precious time on meaningless pursuits—strings of endless romantic relationships, working countless hours at a job in pursuit of the elusive promotion or raise, and the bottomless pit of attaining "enough" money or possessions. Sadly, even Christians do this and I know because I have been guilty myself.

I spent far too many years chasing dreams based in the temporal world, instead of having vision for the eternal one. I wrongly believed that if I started my own successful business and had a great income, then I would feel happy and fulfilled. Thankfully, I eventually realized what Solomon had also concluded when he described in Ecclesiastes 2:11, "Then I looked on all the works that my hands had done and on the labor in which I had toiled; and indeed all was vanity and grasping for the wind. There was no profit under the sun." What happens when a person grasps for the wind? They come up empty-handed every time.

It doesn't have to be that way. In Matthew 6:19-20 Jesus said, "Do not lay up for yourselves treasures on earth, where moth and rust destroy and where thieves break in and steal; but lay up for yourselves treasures in heaven, where neither moth nor rust destroys and where thieves do not break in and steal." In other words, we have a choice: pursue treasures on earth or treasures in heaven.

Let me tell you, there is no greater joy than living a life for Jesus Christ, instead of our own empty ambitions and materialism. To serve God by ministering to people has filled my life with renewed purpose and sustained joy. Laying up treasure in heaven may not always be easy, but it is certainly fulfilling; whereas laying up treasure on this earth is an exercise in futility.

That's because God created us for a specific purpose on this earth to sow seeds for His kingdom. When we do what we were created to do, we are living the life He intended for us to live.

In the poem, the reason I say to "cherish your dreams" is because in many ways your dreams are hidden clues to what God wants to use for His glory, to help you lay up treasures in heaven. God didn't give you those dreams for *your* glory; He gave you those dreams for *His* glory.

Are you a musician? Let God use that gift for His worship. Are you a natural teacher? Then use that gift to spread the gospel. Are you gifted with your hands? Be a servant and help those in need. Do you enjoy cooking? Go feed the hungry. You get the idea! The list of possibilities is endless.

You may be thinking, *Ok, how do I begin submitting my dreams to His will and using my gifts for His glory?* Begin by making that very commitment to God in prayer and ask Him to reveal His will and to show you the way.

I like how Jesus said in John 7:17 that "If anyone wills to do His will, he shall know." God wants to see you fulfill the purposes He created you for. If you are genuinely seeking His direction and will, He's going to reveal it to you and you are going to know if it's of Him or of your own flesh. God definitely has a sense of humor but that doesn't mean He plays silly games.

Tell the Lord that you want to lay up treasures in heaven by submitting your dreams, gifts, goals, ambitions, possessions, and your very existence to Him so that He may use those things for His glory, and watch how God will work through your life!

"Yet you do not have because you do not ask. You ask and do not receive, because you ask amiss, that you may spend it on your pleasures."

James 4:2-3

"Being confident of this very thing, that He who has begun a good work in you will complete it until the day of Jesus Christ."

Philippians 1:6

Idyllwild

From the sanctuaries of ancient secrets
I hear a whisper call my name.
It beckons from oceans of majestic pines
To pass through the Refiner's Flame.

And I know in my heart the time has come
To enter the depths of the trees.
To search my soul, to lose my life
And transcend the warm summer breeze.

But what is within where ears cannot hear
And eyes are too blind to see?
Beyond the meadows of eternal life
Where lords of the earth fall to their knees.

Yet the passion burns like a heavenly fire
That turns fear into restful sleep.
Enter the unknown where dreams become truth
In the majestic shadows of the deep.

So with the Spirit's voice softly singing
Before the King I bow to my knees.
And He reaches down and grasps my hand
As we walk toward the ocean of trees.

If there was ever a geographical place where I continue to hear the Holy Spirit speaking to me the loudest and clearest, for me, that place would be Idyllwild, California.

It's difficult for me to explain how through the years I keep getting drawn back to that little town nestled in the San Jacinto mountain range. I guess it all unknowingly began with a friendship I forged with my sixth grade teacher, Mike Laramie. We became friends mostly because in the sixth grade I really didn't have any friends, so Mike reached out to me and mentored me. Not long after I was in junior high, Mike became senior pastor of a little country church in Idyllwild, aptly named Chapel in the Pines.

Many times through the years, my family would go up to visit Mike, his family, and the church. When I was older I made many journeys there on my own. Whether it was taking weekend spiritual retreats with friends, working one summer at a Christian camp, pre-marital counseling, dedicating my daughter, Skylar, or being discipled by Mike for several years, it seemed that my path always led me back up the mountain to that quaint community.

This poem was inspired by an experience I had one summer when I was about sixteen years old, while I was vacationing with my family in Idyllwild for a weekend. We had rented a small cabin nestled in the woods and I was sitting out on the wood deck playing my guitar. It slowly began to dawn on me that in front of my eyes I could see individual trees, but as my view went further back, each tree merged with the other until the forest was obscured by a wall of pines. It reminded me of standing on the beach and watching each individual wave become part of the entire ocean.

My mind began to wonder what mysteries were hidden within the depths of those ancient trees. What have they seen? Who else has walked there through the ages? It was profound to me that if someone were to take one step at a time they would slowly be swallowed up by the forest; yet, they would always be able to see one step ahead of themselves, but never able to really see the forest as a whole.

It dawned on me that our spiritual journey is very similar to the "ocean of trees." From the perimeter, we can't see more than a few steps in front of us. Yet we'll never know the mysteries within unless we allow ourselves to take those first steps and be enveloped into the forest.

Fear of the unknown can make your feet like lead weights, unable to move forward. But God is calling us to trust Him, to have faith, and step out into the unknown where we can experience His power, miracles, and mysteries. But the first step is ours to take and that is where so many people balk.

As I sat there on the deck, wondering what was behind those ageless trees, I imagined that God was behind that wooden curtain, calling me by name, challenging me to "take the plunge," so to speak. In the poem, after careful consideration, I take His hand and together we walk into the forest of the unknown.

I can tell you that in real life, I have stepped into the unknown many times. It's always scary, but each time you come through, more or less unscathed but always refined, your faith is boosted and it is that much easier to trust God the next time He challenges you to walk in faith.

Faith doesn't come easily to a flawed human being but it is vital to our growth as Christians. I believe this is just one of the reasons why Jesus said in Matthew 18:3 that unless we "become as little children" we can't enter the kingdom of heaven. Little children trust their parents—they have faith. When we take God's hand and step out into the unknown, we are like little children, trusting our heavenly Father.

The scariest part of standing before the forest is always that first step, but once you're in you will always be able to see at least one step at a time. Not the whole picture, just a step at a time. And your life will never be the same.

> "Also I heard the voice of the Lord, saying: 'Whom shall I send, and who will go for us?' Then I said, 'Here am I! Send me.'"
>
> Isaiah 6:8

Sweet Night

In the dusky cloak of evening
When troubles cloud my mind
I gaze up toward the heavens
Where all praise is entwined.

Infinite stars remind me
Of worship and truth held dear.
Listen for the sweet symphony
There's no melody I'd rather hear.

Sweet night, my gentle friend
In your dark, I find the Light.
Humbly I come to share in praise
As all wrong is made right.

Celestial meadows make amends
As sorrow drowns in opaque seas.
There is no pain, there is no grief
Only peaceful tranquility.

Staring up at the face of God
I smile at infinity
As mountains turn to piles of dust
Heaven is right here with me.

Sometimes in our lives it may seem that the problems we face are insurmountable. Have you ever felt that way? I know I have experienced that emotion on many occasions.

In the Bible, when Job was at his lowest, a man named Elihu says to him, "Listen to this, O Job; stand still and consider the wondrous works of God" (Job 37:14). Prior to this statement, Elihu was describing to Job how all of nature, in this context weather patterns (rain, wind, snow, thunder, and lightning), proclaim God's majesty and power.

That is what I experience every time I look up at the stars. I could be dealing with the most difficult circumstances, but when I look up at the heavens all my problems are placed in the proper perspective. When I look up at the endless sky of stars, I'm reminded that my God created them and the entire universe they inhabit. He spoke it into existence and holds it all in place. Why should I feel that my problems are too big for God to handle?

It is awesome to be reminded how our struggles pale in comparison to the vastness of the universe and it is humbling to place our problems in the context of eternity and all the generations that my God and His stars have already presided over. All of a sudden, whatever I am dealing with doesn't seem like it's such an earth-shattering event after all!

Consider also how Elihu tells Job to "stand still." In Hebrew, this phrase can also be translated "to stop moving or doing, to cease." Cease what? To cease worrying, panicking, complaining, and whatever other incalculable efforts we may be exercising in our vain attempt to control the situation. Instead, Elihu says to "stand still and consider the wondrous works of God" and in doing so, the entire situation becomes less insurmountable. It's a powerful reminder that our fleshly desire to manage our trials can actually distract us from worshipping God. Yet when we stop and take the time to worship God, despite our circumstances, something incredible takes place. Just like when we look up at the stars in the night sky, the significance of our problems is greatly diminished.

The stars are ancient and the Creator of those stars has existed long before they were made. What problem could you possibly be facing that He hasn't dealt with a million times before through countless generations? How small our problems truly are in the hands of our enormous God!

The key is to look up! Too often, when we are going through times of trial, we are looking down. God wants us in a position of humility, looking up to Him.

"The heavens declare the glory of God; and the firmament shows His handiwork. Day unto day utters speech, and night unto night reveals knowledge. There is no speech nor language where their voice is not heard. Their line has gone out through all the earth, and their words to the end of the world."

Psalm 19:1-4

Shadowlands

Would the gates of heaven accept me
With a heart as twisted as mine?
I am a kingdom without a king
A fool drunk with Death's wine.

My soul is at odds within itself
Haunted by the shadows of my past.
Ominous voices beckon me to that dismal place
Where only the wicked may pass.

Hate is the blood that courses through my veins
And death is the life that it brings.
Encompassed by rage I claw at my grave
While above me I hear mourners sing.

I once was a spirit of light
But now I'm a specter of death.
Alone I roam this desolate earth
Where your pain is my life's breath.

As I gaze upon the sands of time
I see my dreams slip through my hands.
Allow me to taste the fruit of heaven again
That I may escape the shadowlands.

My God has been ever faithful
For it is I who betrayed myself.

I believed the lie that I was in charge
And put my Savior up on a shelf.

Would the gates of heaven accept me
With a heart as shattered as mine?
I am trapped in a lonely grave
Created by my own design.

The "shadowlands" have always been my way of describing a very real place where many Christians wander if they walk away from the Lord at some point in their journey. It is a place of darkness, loneliness, and sorrow, where we are confronted with our inadequacies and weaknesses. It is a place where many Christians find themselves because it is there in the shadowlands that we find out who we truly are and what we really need. In other words, it is a place of testing. It is there that our character and our faith are put to the test.

It was at a time in my life, during college, when I had slowly drifted away from God, that I was inspired to describe my emotions as I walked through my own personal shadowlands. It was easy following God when I was in a Christian school because my faith was strengthened by the environment and people around me. Once I graduated, however, I learned that in college or at work, no one was going to challenge me spiritually or keep me accountable. The depth of my walk with God was dependent on the effort I put in or failed to put in—it would be as shallow or deep as I hungered for it to be. It was little compromises that led me to the shadowlands.

At first I was shocked at the subtle changes that had covered my life like a dark shroud. I was angry, even hateful, and I felt so lost. I hadn't turned my back completely on God, but I wasn't trying to seek Him out either. The separation was unbearable; yet, I refused to allow myself to submit to what I knew was right.

The most painful part of the shadowlands was the loss of the inexplicable joy I once had in life. It is awful to have walked so closely and intimately with God, only to find yourself at a place where you feel abandoned by Him. Only He doesn't abandon any of us, it's we who abandon Him. That is what I meant when I begged to be allowed to "taste the fruit of heaven again." It is the proverbial cry of the Prodigal Son as he finds himself eating out of the pig trough. The irony of that parable, of course, much like the irony of real life, is that we can leave that pig pen whenever we want to, yet it is our own pride and stubbornness that keeps us there.

In hindsight, I believe that for many of us it is in the shadowlands where we make our final decision about how we are going to live our lives. It is a place of questioning, where each person must decide whether they are going to follow Christ or the world.

Either a person comes out of this time with their faith stronger and intact or it breaks them and they abandon all that they once believed. Jesus wants people to live for Him because they really want to, not because they are obligated or because they think that a Christian life is just about selfishly feeling good.

When I finally chose to come back from my personal shadowlands, I had learned what an imperfect, fallible creature I am; yet, despite my innumerable shortcomings, I am a loved and cherished child of God. I also learned just how faithful God truly is despite our own unfaithfulness.

There is nothing we can ever do that will ever "earn" us God's love or salvation. Just like my children don't earn my love, they just have it, so God's love for us also is a free gift that we just have to accept. However, before we can accept it, we must get over ourselves. We must be humble enough to accept His love and lordship over our lives.

God loved me before I ever loved Him and because of that I am able to love Him in return.

"Yea, though I walk through the valley of the shadow of death, I will fear no evil; for You are with me."

Psalm 23:4

Company of Wolves

There was a time when joy transcended fear
And hope was the breath of the soul.

The future was more than a pleasant dreamscape
It was a window of unspoken joy.

There was no silent sadness
Every shadow encompassed by love bred hope.

Yet the quagmire of futility is silently suffocating
The hopes and dreams of innocence.

Do you wish to breathe that sweet aroma again?
And bask in the fields of fading darkness?

I feel loneliness running with the company of wolves
As silence fades the joy.

Have you ever felt as if you were waiting on the verge of some undiscovered purpose in your life, while at the same time feeling like some elusive final piece of the puzzle was somehow within your grasp, yet nowhere to be found? I'm sure you have.

I believe that all people were created by God to live a life of significance. We are not called to a life of mediocrity and selfish indulgence, but a life where God's light can shine through us for the entire dark world to see.

The problem is that most people never discover the purpose for their existence. Some believe lies that they are insignificant, worthless, and meaningless. They think that perceived shortcomings, such as a lack of education, age, or their background, excludes them from being used by God. Others have no interest in discovering their purpose simply because they are preoccupied with living in the moment. Life to them is simply a pattern of self-centered behavior. They have no interest in the meaning of life; they just take for granted the reason they are here.

Some people do realize that they were born with a purpose, yet they forever stand on the outskirts. They choose to stand on the outside looking in, afraid to take the next step out of their comfort zone. Sadly, it's not uncommon for such a person to look back on their life with regret, always wondering what could have been.

Then there are those who not only realize their God-given significance, but they embrace it too! They step out of their comfort zone, set aside their selfish desires, bravely face their obstacles and weaknesses, and march head-on into the purpose for which they were created.

As I look at the people who I pass throughout life, I can't help but observe that many people never reach that level of meaning in their lives. How do I know? I can see it on their faces. If eyes really are the window to one's soul, then what I often see in one's soul is emptiness.

I wrote this poem at a time in my life when I felt that I had once been on the path to living God's purpose for my life, but because of sin, I had lost the trail. I repented of my sin and asked God for forgiveness, but I couldn't forgive myself. I held onto my feelings of self-condemnation for a long time. My obstacle was named Guilt and I allowed it to control my life so that I had begun to believe that I had ruined any purpose that God had created for me. I lived in this defeated mindset for many years, believing the lies that I was worthless and not good enough.

Does that describe how you feel right now? If it does, I have good news for you! Once God forgives you, there is no need to condemn yourself anymore. Holding onto your guilt after you have been forgiven is only pride disguised as false humility. It becomes a crutch, an excuse for inaction. It is a way of attempting to cover up the fear we feel as we cower and lick our wounds. Believe me, there is nothing Satan would want more then to permanently cripple a person into that type of mindset for the rest of their life.

But it doesn't have to be that way. It says in the book of Psalms that as far as the east is from the west, that's how far God will remove our sins from us. Have you considered how far apart east and west are on a straight line? They go on for infinity in separate directions. That means our sins are ancient history.

If you have made mistakes like me, and I'm sure you have, don't allow yourself to become debilitated by them. I wasted too many years of my life believing the lie that I was no longer worthy to live out the plan God has for me. I have news for you—none of us are worthy even on our absolute best day! But God loves us anyway. So ask God for forgiveness, allow Him to help pick you up off the ground, and keep pressing forward. Go live that life of significance that God specifically created you to live.

"As far as the east is from the west, so far has He removed our transgressions from us."

Psalm 103:12

Innocent Surrender

As spikes of green grasped at the last blades of light
A monument appeared in the haze
Ancient with the hopes of unnumbered before.

The etched script read dim
But was illuminated from above
As fireflies danced out swirling beats of light.

They spotted what I wanted to say
And yet I knew things were as they always should be
A curious imbalance of known and yet to come.

In wonderment the illumination spread
To the very depths of my spirit
To the place where truth becomes the light of breaking day.

The etched script, ancient with hopes and dreams
Reflected the vision of my soul
Like moonlight on the waves of time.

I am now faced with the mysterious unknown
That secret place where dreams and reality merge into one
Such a curious place to be—seeing by faith.

Yet despite the mystery there is an underlying certainty
That I am not alone on this untraversed path
Leading to a place both unknown yet familiar.

Peace floods my soul
Saturating me with the hope of ancients
Singing His melodic memories.

This monument, this beacon in a world of despair
It is love saved from the beginning of eternity
For such a time as this.

I've always been fascinated by the "curious imbalance of known and yet to come." In my mind, this is a vital part of a lifelong walk with Jesus Christ. In our flesh, our human nature, we of course long to understand everything and to know what our future holds for us. Yet faith requires us to not be able to see the entire picture.

One of my favorite scriptures in the Bible says, "Your word is a lamp to my feet and a light to my path." I grew up with Psalm 119:105 in the form of an old worship song, but it wasn't until I was an adult that the subtle meaning behind the wording began to sink in.

I realized that a "lamp to my feet" doesn't illuminate the entire path before me; it only shows me one step at a time. That is where faith comes in. If we knew everything that was before us, why would we need to trust in God? Yet it is by learning to trust and be dependent on Him that we slowly die to ourselves. That is why faith is such an important element of growing as a Christian. It is why another one of my favorite scriptures, Hebrews 11:6 says, "But without faith it is impossible to please Him, for he who comes to God must believe that He is, and that He is a rewarder of those who diligently seek Him." Imagine that! Without faith it is *impossible* to please God.

Now, I'm not saying I don't struggle with this—I am still an imperfect human being in a fallen world after all—but I must admit that I am learning to be more at peace with trusting in God to lead and guide my life.

I heard someone once use the analogy of riding a roller coaster for the first time to describe the uncertainty of life. When you are on the ride, you have no idea what is around the next turn. It could be a rise, loop, a drop—you name it! And in all of it you are frightened and excited, screaming and laughing! I love roller coasters and I can attest that riding one for the first time is the most fun because you just don't know what is going to happen next.

I hope this poem encourages you to grasp onto the uncertainty of life and just enjoy hanging on for the ride because though it can often be a harrowing experience, we do have one certainty—that we will never walk the path alone. Through every step of the way, we have our loving Savior to guide us and to lead us through the difficult times.

So embrace the unknown. For it is in the unknown that Jesus makes Himself known; it is in the uncertainty that He becomes our certainty.

"And lo, I am with you always, even to the end of the age."

Matthew 28:20

The Canopy of Leaves

Have you ever dreamed what I have dreamed?
Passing under the canopy of leaves, sunlight flickering
Shadowy veils dancing in the wind.
All is not what it seems as our eyes lock, unknowing.

Who is this angel before me?
I touch her elegant hands, heavenly light
Soft as the stillness of a quiet stream.
Curious eyes from distant lands reflect childlike innocence.

What secrets are held in a heart so pure?
Her eyes betray thoughts within, mirrors of her soul
Candles reflecting dreams of ethereal light.
I want to gaze within, to know such dreams and visions.

Would she permit me to follow?
Angel, please take me to that secret place
Where heaven's truth is revealed.
I release her elegant hands; her gaze is pure innocence.

When I was a child, I remember a picture that used to hang in my younger brother's bedroom. It was a picture of two children crossing a rickety old bridge while a guardian angel stood over them with protective arms outstretched. As a child, whenever I looked at that picture it would fill me with a sense of both wonder and peace.

This poem describes a scene in which I meet an angel face-to-face. No doubt like many of you, I have had situations in my life that I am confident some type of angelic intervention was involved. I have often wondered (and prayed) for angelic protection, especially over my children. I've even wondered if, like the picture in my brother's room, we all have lifelong guardian angels.

When I was a teenager, I remember rear-ending a car on my way to youth group one night. I wasn't paying close attention and when I saw the other car stopped in front of me, it was too late. I slammed on the brakes! I heard the tires screeching, I saw the look of fear in the driver's reflection in his rearview mirror, then the impact. My heart sank because I was driving my parents' car and I was a newly minted driver. Not knowing for sure what to do, I decided to get out of my car and talk with the other driver. The person was certainly scared and quite shaken up, but he said that I hadn't actually hit him. He felt no impact and there was no damage to either car. Yet I know I hit *something* because I heard it and felt it. I remember getting back in my car, breathing a sigh of relief, and praising God for His angelic protection.

God's Word is clear that angels do exist and they are most certainly involved in the lives of mankind, but the Bible doesn't explicitly state that we have angels who are assigned specifically to protect us on a constant watch.

That is probably for the best that we don't know for sure. After all, humanity has enough "idols" that need to be cleaned out from our lives as it is. If guardian angels were a known fact, then there would be the danger that people would worship them and not God.

It's important to remember that God is the one in control, not angels, or us. He chooses to use angels to do His will, much like He chooses us; yet, He is more than capable of accomplishing His work without us. That is why it is such a humbling realization to know that God chooses to use imperfect, flawed vessels like us to spread the gospel message and to do His kingdom's work on this earth. That is an amazing honor and a privilege—one that should never be taken for granted. That truth should always lead us to worship Him and nothing else.

So whether or not we have guardian angels doesn't really matter. What does matter is that angels serve at the pleasure of our heavenly Father and it is He who is omniscient, omnipresent, and omnipotent, not the angels. He is more than capable to act on our behalf without them. As David proclaimed in Psalm 18:2, "The Lord is my rock and my fortress and my deliverer; my God, my strength, in whom I will trust; my shield and the horn of my salvation, my stronghold."

Still, just like the poem, it's fun to speculate. Obviously angels have captured the imagination of humanity, even non-believers, going all the way back to ancient times. Nevertheless, we must never forget that it is our God who is really running the show!

> "For the eyes of the Lord run to and fro throughout the whole earth, to show Himself strong on behalf of those whose heart is loyal to Him."
>
> 2 Chronicles 16:9

Suspended in Autumn

The setting sun simply fades away
Like future dreams that have gone astray.
The storm clouds of autumn begin to roll in
Suffocating my visions of summer innocence.

Piercing darkness envelopes my soul
Like waves crashing on a distant shore.
Where moonless skies kiss black seas below
And I feel the fearsome swells within me.

Yet through the darkness of the opaque night
A hint of love makes all wrongs right.
Such innocent joy transforms the night sky
Into rays of splendor on the oceans of time.

Heal these dreams of distant memories.
A soft kiss on the cheek would more than please
A weary traveler like me, to ease the pain
Of many dreams lost, but more to gain.

I can feel the winds of change blowing passionately
Through the depths of my soul, so powerfully.
And I know to hold you in my arms would calm my fears
Of fleeting time and passing years.

So take my hand, sweet spirit of light
And may our dreams and joys take flight.

Even at a young age, I always seemed to be looking for my bride. I was never able to be fully content with the joys of life because I always had a longing to share them with someone special. Usually this realization would hit me in those moments that were the most beautiful, such as watching the moonlight reflect off the ocean's waves, or seeing ominous clouds roll across the sky warning of the impending storm. In those moments, I would wish for someone to share those experiences with. So it was a shock to me after years of failed searching for that someone who would love and understand me that I met the woman I would one day marry in the most unexpected place.

In 1998, Juanita and I both happened to be working at the same job, but in different departments. I noticed her right away because she was beautiful and had the type of personality that would draw people to her, like moths to a flame. I was smitten.

After many months of attempting, even begging her to agree to go on a first date with me, she finally relented. It was the month of August when we went on our first date to Knott's Berry Farm and after that we were inseparable.

It didn't take long for me to realize that I wanted to spend the rest of my life with her. The problem was that we had only been together for a few months and I didn't want to scare her. So being the pillar of self-control that I am, I proceeded to bring up "marriage" to which she was surprisingly in agreement with me!

But things started to go too fast and soon I found my summer dream unraveling with the chill of autumn as she slowly began to pull away from me. It seemed like God was playing a cruel joke when Juanita asked me to give her space to clear her head. Of course, I was devastated.

I wrote this poem during that time when it seemed that all I had asked and prayed for all my life had just slipped through my fingers and all but disappeared. I had no choice but to give the entire situation over to God, trusting that He loved me and would deliver me from the valley I was wandering in. You see, it is a poem of loss but also of hope. Although I was crushed, I never lost hope.

I realized through that experience that often in our lives God will appear to take something dear away from us for a season because He is testing our faith. Sometimes He even takes it away forever. But I learned that if you really love Him, you have to be willing to let it all go. He must come first and everything else must be a distant second. That is what Jesus was talking about when He said in Matthew 16:24-25 that "If anyone desires to come after Me, let him deny himself, and take up his cross, and follow Me. For whoever desires to save his life will lose it, but whoever loses his life for My sake will find it." When I finally gave my hopes and dreams to Him, that's when He brought me my bride.

Looking back at that experience, I know that my marriage to Juanita and my relationship with God are much stronger now because we all weathered that storm together.

"Every good and perfect gift is from above, and comes down from the Father of lights, with whom there is no variation or shadow of turning."

James 1:17

"If you then, being evil, know how to give good gifts to your children, how much more will your Father who is in heaven give good things to those who ask Him!"

Matthew 7:11

Heavenly Father

You are a hope to the hopeless
A strength for those who are weak.
You defend those who are helpless
You protect those who are meek.

You are a rest to the burdened
A shelter when there's nowhere to sleep.
You are a gentle spring to the thirsty
You are a joy for those who weep.

You are a father to the fatherless
A comfort in times of fright.
You are a daddy to the lonely child,
You are his guardian in the night.

I remember being a young child, waking up from a bad dream, getting up out of bed, and going out into the hallway to see if anyone else was awake. Most of the time all the lights in the house were off, signifying that everyone else was fast asleep, except one was always on. The light to my dad's study downstairs was like a beacon in the darkness of the night.

Just knowing that my father was awake and working in his study always gave me a sense of peace and comfort. I knew that while he was awake, he was always looking out for us and protecting us. Sometimes I would go downstairs to talk to him, but most of the time I just went right back to bed. All my fears were gone and I felt safe once again.

Our heavenly Father is the same way. Psalm 121:3-4 says, "He will not allow your foot to be moved; He who keeps you will not slumber. Behold, He who keeps Israel shall neither slumber nor sleep." He is always standing guard, watching over us. He is a constant source of comfort, a refuge when the storms of life seem to be about to wash us away in their currents. In a similar way that an earthly father looks out for the interests of his children, God, so much more so, is always looking out for us.

Now, as a father myself, I have a better understanding of how much my heavenly Father loves me. After all, if my earthly father, who is only a mortal man loves me the way he does, and knowing how much I love my own children, though I am imperfect, how much more so does my perfect

Father in heaven love me? It's a beautiful picture that staggers my imagination!

"God is our refuge and strength, a very present help in trouble. Therefore we will not fear, even though the earth be removed, and though the mountains be carried into the midst of the sea."

Psalm 46:1-2

"I will not leave you nor forsake you."

Joshua 1:5

The Secluded Meadow

Last night in a moonlit forest
They danced in my dreams.
Inside a secluded meadow
Beside heavenly streams.

And the angels sang love songs
As they soared high above.
While two lives joined together
In my dream as in their love.

And as twilight began to descend
He gazed into her eyes.
As he held her in his arms
Amidst the forest's sighs.

And when they kissed, so pure
The angels began to sing
Of love that never dies
And dreams that summer nights bring.

The Father smiled that evening
As they danced in my dreams.
Inside a secluded meadow
Beside heavenly streams.

One thing that always puts a smile on my face is when I see an older married couple still having fun and excited to be together, even after all those years. I can only imagine all the storms and obstacles they have weathered together, and all the joyful memories they've shared. I know it couldn't have been easy, but they remained faithful to their commitment. That is such a beautiful accomplishment.

The day that I wrote this poem I was imagining a couple, alone in a forest, just enjoying each other's company. I pictured them in a quiet secret place, away from all the cares of life, just celebrating their relationship, while God approvingly watched them dance. I know it may seem a little corny to some, but I'm a romantic at heart and I just love the setting and imagery. It reminds me that any truly successful marriage has to have Jesus Christ as its center and foundation.

Ecclesiastes 4:9-12 states, "Two are better than one, because they have a good reward for their labor. For if they fall, one will lift up his companion. But woe to him who is alone when he falls, for he has no one to help him up. Again, if two lie down together, they will keep warm; but how can one be warm alone? Though one may be overpowered by another, two can withstand him. And a threefold cord is not quickly broken."

I love how King Solomon, the author of these words, points out the practical importance of relationships. The truth is that God never intended for us to be alone, but rather to share our lives with others. This brings us back to the most important human relationship you will ever have—the one between you and your spouse.

In Solomon's example, we see the practical benefits of not being alone. As a couple we can work together and accomplish tasks twice as fast, we can care for one another through times of injury or illness, meet each other's emotional, spiritual, and physical needs, as well as defend and protect one another. In other words, life is so much easier when we have a partner to help us!

This is what God was saying in Genesis 2:18 when He states, "It is not good that man should be alone; I will make him a helper comparable to him."

But it is Solomon's statement in verse 12 that strikes me the most and inspired this poem. He speaks of the threefold cord that is not quickly broken. We've all seen rope which is actually comprised of other ropes all wound tightly together. It doesn't take much imagination to understand why a threefold cord is much stronger than a twofold or a single cord. But here's the fascinating point: in the previous two verses we read about the relationship between two people, which would equate to a twofold cord. So who is the third cord? It is God.

When we weave our marriages together with a relationship with Jesus Christ, a foundation is created that is infinitely stronger than if we tried to sustain the relationship without Him. A threefold cord can withstand a lot more pressure and pulling than a twofold cord.

So if you want your marriage to be stronger, so that you can experience all the benefits of your relationship to the fullest, as well as successfully weather the storms of life together with your marriage intact, be sure not to leave God out!

"So then, they are no longer two but one flesh. Therefore what God has joined together, let not man separate."

Matthew 19:6

"Therefore a man shall leave his father and mother and be joined to his wife, and they shall become one flesh."

Genesis 2:24

April

As I dream I can hear her name in the wind
The memory and the dream seem unreal.
The past is nothing but a distant memory.
As I watch the past is concealed.

Was it a dream or was there a time
When we both laughed and played?
When life was ours like a fruit to be plucked
Yet the wind is her voice that won't stay.

Why can't I remember her name?
The wind blows in my face with a start.
Its chill burns right through me
And I feel a sharp pain in my heart.

She comes face to face with me
And I look deep into her hollow eyes.
Only innocence lost and despair found
As I watch a teardrop fall from her eyes.

I reach to her but she dashes away
For almost a moment I know her.
I catch her tear as the wind whips her away
Only a memory of what we once were.

Interestingly, this is the very first poem I ever wrote, back in 1991 when I was a sophomore in high school. Unfortunately, this poem was inspired by a dear friend of mine who had once been completely on fire for Jesus, yet walked away to enter into a dating relationship with a popular guy on campus who did not share her spiritual convictions. The slow slide of compromise was indiscernible at first; yet, just like in the poem, a moment did come when we came face-to-face and I no longer recognized my friend. At the time, I remember wondering aloud to God how something like this could happen so easily.

James 1:14-15 says, "But each one is tempted when he is drawn away by his own desires and enticed. Then, when desire has conceived, it gives birth to sin; and sin, when it is full-grown, brings forth death." In other words, it is the little compromises that lead to bigger compromises later on. Most people don't fall on their face in a day; it's a slow decline, like quicksand, and they are swallowed up in sin before they know it.

We need to be honest with ourselves about how susceptible we all are to slowly falling into sin. There is a war going on around us and in us between our fleshly desires and the Holy Spirit. We need to be careful not to give our enemy even an inch because Satan will exploit any opportunity he can. That is why Paul wrote in First Timothy 6:11, "But you, O man of God, flee these things and pursue righteousness, godliness, faith, love, patience, gentleness."

The good news is that though Satan's methods may change, his strategy remains the same. Going all the way back to the garden, he first puts doubt into people's minds about the validity of God's Word, and once that has taken root the rest is usually downhill.

Listen, the enemy wants to make us believe we can get close to the fire without getting burned. Yet, like the frog in the slow-boiling pot, we often realize too late that we're not standing *near* the fire; instead, we are burning *in* it. Or think of it another way—the closer you dance to the edge of a cliff, the more likely you are to trip and fall over it.

Let me encourage you (as I also encourage myself), stay strong in your faith, stay rooted in the Word, and do not allow even a foothold for sin to take root. When that thought of sinful possibility even enters your mind, do as Paul said in Second Corinthians 10:5 and bring "every thought into captivity to the obedience of Christ."

"How can a young man cleanse his way? By taking heed according to Your word. With my whole heart I have sought You; oh, let me not wander from Your commandments! Your word I have hidden in my heart, that I might not sin against You."

Psalm 119:9-11

The Night Terror

One night in a silent slumber
I had a dream like none before.
A dream that I was a part of.
A nightmare of forgotten lore.

My world began to suffocate.
In darkness I began to see.
Now listen close to what I say
For this is what happened to me.

I lay on the beach listening
As the thunder rolls overhead.
Torrents of rain crash upon me
While the ocean gives up its dead.

I watch the bodies howl and moan
As the earth trembles with their cries.
The waves begin to roll and foam
While ominous clouds fill the skies.

I feel the fear deep within me
As the air becomes dense with death.
And I lay there trembling in fear
While I choke on the ocean's breath.

I twist and turn moving nowhere
As my blood rushes with the ride.

I feel my fear grow within me
While the spirits rise with the tide.

I open my mouth to speak the name of Christ
But my voice is muffled in the din.
Yet the power of His name cannot be contained
As His light cleanses the dark of its sin.

I know I dream in a conscious state
As I feel them scream in my face.
With wonder I open my eyes
While they vanish without a trace.

I lay on the beach surrounded by peace
Basking in the glow of the sun.
One last chill crawls across my skin.
The war has just begun!

I often look back on that night
For it still lingers in my dreams.
It threatens me with sheer terror
As I hear their silent screams.

After reading this poem, you may think that it is merely symbolic. In a way, you'd be correct, but not entirely. You may be surprised to know that something really did happen to me one summer night before my senior year in high school, which inspired this poem.

The day began with a visit to my youth pastor. Jeff was like a big brother to us kids and his guidance and teaching had proved invaluable to my personal spiritual development. On this particular afternoon, I was meeting with Jeff to discuss my upcoming role as worship leader on campus.

Years have faded my memory a bit regarding the actual details of the conversation, but I do remember that Jeff had cracked open a spiritual door on the subject of worship and allowed me a glimpse inside. What I saw was so powerful and overwhelming, it actually stunned me. I left his office that day excited but also extremely respectful of the responsibility I was about to face.

That night I had a dream. I don't remember falling asleep. I just remember my mind turning on like a television set. In my dream, I was in the mountains driving on a winding road which disappeared behind the ocean of trees. I realized I had slammed on the brakes of my car because I had almost hit someone who had suddenly crossed the road. As I took in my surroundings, I realized that I was in Idyllwild. Somehow in my dream, I was aware that I had left Jeff's office, fallen asleep, and miraculously driven into the mountains.

I woke up in a sudden fright. You know the feeling. Your heart is beating right out of your chest and for a few moments of disorientation you have no idea what is real and what isn't. After a few seconds, I realized I was in my bedroom and none of the dream had been real. With a breath of relief, I allowed myself to relax back into bed as I replayed that dream in my mind's eye once again. That's when the real nightmare began.

Instantly, I felt a real physical weight land on my back, pinning me facedown to the bed. There are no words to adequately describe the noises I heard or the fear I felt. Suffice it to say that I heard all Hell break loose in my room. I heard screaming and wailing, sirens and chaos all around. I tried to lift my body up out of bed so I could run out of my room as quickly as possible, but the weight on my back was too much. It wasn't a crushing weight, but it was leveraged on me in such a way that I was powerless to move against it. I instinctively knew that I was under spiritual attack and I had to cry out the name of Jesus, so I began to pray out loud, but a pressure (which felt alarmingly like a hand) clamped over my mouth.

I tried not to panic and even though I was scared out of my wits, I began to pray in my mind. My prayer rebuked the enemy in the name and authority of Jesus Christ and after what seemed like an eternity, the pressure on my mouth and back began to lessen, and the noises began to slowly die away. As soon as I was able, I pushed myself out of bed, opened the door, and bolted out into the hallway.

The house was dead silent as I gazed into the shadows of my room. My siblings were fast asleep and my parents were out visiting friends. Slowly, I went back into the room, turned on the lights, put on some worship music, and opened my Bible to pray.

I could still feel a slight lingering presence of fear in my room. I could feel it passing over my body in waves. Then just as the last of the fear was gone, I heard the following phrase whispered in my ear—*the war has just begun*. I sat there in bed, unable to fall back asleep for some time, pondering the meaning of those five simple words.

It has been many years since that summer night and the night terror I had, but those words have never left my subconscious mind. They represent a threat, intimidation, and yet also a challenge. There is a choice that each of us must make at some point in our lives, and the choice is this: will we take an active part in the spiritual war that surrounds us each day or will we cower in fear, intimidated, and afraid to go further in our spiritual journey?

If you are at a place in your life where it seems that the enemy is trying to scare or intimidate you, take heart! You're probably doing something right!

"For we do not wrestle against flesh and blood, but against principalities, against powers, against the rulers of the darkness of this age, against spiritual hosts of wickedness in the heavenly places. Therefore take up the whole armor of God, that you may be able to withstand in the evil day, and having done all, to stand."

Ephesians 6:12-13

"Perfect love casts out fear."

1 John 4:18

"You must not fear them, for the Lord your God Himself fights for you."

Deuteronomy 3:22

Skylar's Lullaby

You hear the cry of your daughter far away.
You are nearby as she lays for sleep.
You hold the stars as the light fades to night.
You bring peace to her soul as You sing her to sleep.

She wakes in the night to a gentle breathing.
You are the wind blowing her cares away.
She rests in You as You are singing
"Come find peace in Me. I am the only way."

The daylight breaks, the morning rings
Your child awakes as she hears You sing.
"Come find rest in Me. I will make your burden light.
Come find peace for your soul. Let your heart take flight."

Your daughter comes to You, just as the break of day.
She knows You love her in every way.

As far back as I can remember I always looked forward to one day becoming a dad. I remember when I was in junior high I began collecting baseball cards, not for myself, but for my future son. I also began coming up with names for my daughter. Don't ask me how I knew at 12 years old that one day in the future I would have both a son and a daughter, but I did.

Flash forward to September 2003, when half of my dream came true and my gorgeous daughter, Skylar, was born. I still remember when I held her against my chest for the first time. There is this classic photo we have (it's actually the first picture taken of the two of us together) with her swaddled in a blanket and me holding her up for the camera as if she were a trophy. The truth is Skylar is far better than a trophy, she is a priceless treasure, a gift, and I am honored to have the privilege of being her dad.

A few days after we had brought our newborn daughter home from the hospital, she was lying in our bed and it hit me for the first time that Skylar was more than just a baby. In that little body lay a lifetime of potential. I was filled with joy at the prospect of getting to know this "little person" that was now lying so helpless in our bed. What would be her personality, hobbies, opinions, thoughts, career, dreams, and goals? What a treat to spend the rest of my life discovering this gift from God.

Becoming a dad has given me such a deeper appreciation for how God views His children. It baffles me to know that as much as I love my children, it is nothing compared to how much God loves His little ones. I'm a flawed man with many shortcomings. He is the perfect Creator of the universe. I love my kids, but He invented love; in fact, He *is* love.

Just as a good dad is readily available to come to the aid of his children, our heavenly Father is always there for us. And unlike a human father, who will inevitably fail at some point, our heavenly Father is perfect and will never fail us. Jesus said in Matthew 7:9-11, "Or what man is there among you who, if his son asks for bread, will give him a stone? Or if he asks for a fish, will he give him a serpent? If you then, being evil, know how to give good gifts to your children, how much more will your Father who is in heaven give good things to those who ask Him?"

As much as I love Skylar, I know I can never give her as much as Jesus can give her. That was the thought behind this poem. I imagined her, some night in the future, alone and crying herself to sleep. For whatever reason in the poem, I'm either unaware of her pain or just not able to resolve it. But where man is limited and powerless, our God is unlimited and powerful, and so it is He who comes to her aid and comfort.

God appointed me to be Skylar's dad and I praise Him every day for this calling, but ultimately Skylar is in His hands because she belongs to Him. The same is true for each one of us who can call ourselves His children. What a comfort to be in the hands of a loving God and Father!

"I will lift up my eyes to the hills—from whence comes my help? My help comes from the Lord, who made heaven and earth. He will not allow your foot to be moved; He who keeps you will not slumber. Behold, He who keeps Israel shall neither slumber nor sleep. The Lord is your keeper; the Lord is your shade at your right hand. The sun shall not strike you by day, nor the moon by night. The Lord shall preserve you from all evil; He shall preserve your soul. The Lord shall preserve your going out and your coming in from this time forth, and even forevermore."

Psalm 121

"The Lord is my rock and my fortress and my deliverer; my God, my strength, in whom I will trust; my shield and the horn of my salvation, my stronghold."

Psalm 18:2

Sereja

I remember the night my grandfather died.

I lay asleep in bed, dreaming dreams not yet spoken of.
Thoughts as innocent and warm as the gentle breeze
That swept through my open window.

I remember a soft tapping at my bedroom door.
As the door opened, flooding my room
With the soft ethereal light from the hallway
I heard my mother's soft voice whisper
"Erik, your grandfather just passed away."

As I lay with moonlight cascading through my window
I wept.
Why hadn't I been there?

I suddenly remembered my promise
To play him a song on my guitar.
Every time he saw me he would ask me to sing.
I can still hear myself saying
"Next time I am here, I will play my guitar.
Next time, I will sing you a song.
Next time."
I never did.

I thought of this man that I knew so little about.
He came from the Soviet Union without anything

Except his cherished family.
He was a hard worker, a fighter
A survivor of wars.
He overcame imprisonment in Siberia
Genocide in Armenia and persecution wherever he went.
He was a revolutionary from another generation.

I remember the sadness in his eyes.
Pain was his constant companion.

I remembered how he would eagerly wait by the front door
When my family was coming to visit.
When he would lean forward to kiss me on the cheek
His faced seemed so rough compared to mine.
Yet even though his body had become weak in old age
His eyes still emanated the strength of his youth.
"I have survived, I have overcome!"

I remembered the stories my dad told me as a child.
How my grandfather fled from country to country.
How he was thrown in prison because of his faith in God.
And how his only dream was to find freedom in America.
Although he did find that freedom
He also found more hardship.

Yet in the midst of struggles
My grandfather was rarely alone.
He saved lives and helped feed many hungry immigrants.
He was never at a loss for friends.
He was considered by many to be a guardian angel.

My grandfather understood the meaning of life.
He knew what mattered most of all.
He gave his life as a living sacrifice to God
His family, his friends, and his new country.

He refused to give up.
Standing firm against adversity, he was a pillar of hope.
In the face of trials and pain, he never backed down.
He fought to protect his family.
He fought to protect me.

When he died I suffered a heavy loss
But out of that loss grew an admiration
And a love that I had never appreciated before.

As I stood at his funeral
Watching the single white rose I had placed on his casket
I began to understand who and what I was called to be.
I am a living reminder of my grandfather's legacy.
I am his words, I am his breath.
His story of personal sacrifice and faith will live on
Through me and through my children.
It is etched on our hearts and it shall not be forgotten.

And I wept.

Looking back on my life, there are a handful of decisions I have made that I would happily reverse, if I could. Thankfully, most of my errors in judgment have all been positive learning experiences that have taught me profound spiritual lessons. Yet there is one decision I once made that, if given the choice, I would take back in an instant and that has to do with the night my grandfather passed away.

I was never particularly close with any of my grandparents. My mom's father passed away before I was born and her mother passed away when I was only a toddler. I did have a relationship with my dad's parents but it was an awkward one because they weren't your typical grandparents.

I have this one memory, as a little boy, when my grandmother took me Christmas shopping at the mall. My heart's desire was a new G.I. Joe tank that had recently hit the toy store shelves. When I showed it to her in the shop window and asked her to buy it for me, I was stunned at how angry she got and her refusal to purchase the toy. In the mind of a seven-year-old, I remember being aware at the time that all my friend's grandparents seemed to buy them anything they requested; after all, wasn't that what grandparents were supposed to do? It wasn't until I later grew up that I realized there was nothing whimsical about "toy" tanks to my grandparents. In their lifetime, they had witnessed real tanks obliterating people, utterly destroying property, raining down ruin and destruction. It was a point of reference that, as a child, I neither understood nor appreciated. In other words, I didn't relate to my grandparents, so I wasn't as close to them growing up as I wish I could have been.

My grandmother passed away first, not long after I graduated from high school. Ironically, my family had visited them for dinner the night she died and she had specifically asked for me. I was spending the night at a friend's house when I got the call. I remember realizing for the first time that life truly is short and our time with loved ones is not guaranteed. I decided to spend more time with my grandfather, since he was the only grandparent I had left. Of course, as a selfish teenager I did the exact opposite and hardly saw my grandfather over the next few months.

I remember the day my aunt called my mom to tell her that something was wrong with my grandfather. He had lost partial control over half his body, a sure sign of a stroke. I was doing college homework in my room when my mom came to ask me if I would go with her to see what was wrong. I dutifully told her that I had to finish my work for class the next day. So she went without me. It's with bitter irony that I don't even remember the name of the class I chose over my grandfather.

When she finally got home later that day, she told me that she had to carry him to the car to get him to the hospital, but that he was all right at the moment. I remember sadly thinking that if I had gone with her, I could have been the one to carry him to the car. When we all went to bed that night, I had already made the decision that

I would go visit him in the hospital on my way to class first thing the next morning.

We were all asleep when the phone rang and we got that dreaded call to come down to the hospital quickly because he wasn't going to last much longer. My mom knocked on my bedroom door and asked me to come with the family. In a semiconscious state I told her that I needed my rest and that I would visit him early in the morning. So they left without me.

I don't remember the details of my peaceful dreaming, only that the next thing I knew my mom was again knocking at my door, telling me that they had just returned from the hospital and that my grandfather had passed away.

I looked over at my alarm clock and realized that it was less than an hour before I would've woken up to get ready to go see him on my way to school. And that's when it hit me. I had been given two separate opportunities that day to be with my grandfather in his final hours. When he was too weak to walk, I could have carried him. When he was dying in bed, I could have said goodbye. Instead, I had squandered both opportunities for reasons that were insignificant and shallow. That is why I wept.

My grandfather died six months to the exact day that my grandmother passed away. My father told me that after she was gone, my grandfather would just sit on a little plastic lawn chair in the living room and watch the cars drive by through the window. He probably passed away from loneliness just as much as the stroke. I wouldn't have known though because I utterly failed to see him during those months after her funeral.

The day my grandfather was buried I went to the mortuary hours earlier than anyone else, before the casket was closed and transported to his burial site. I brought my guitar with me and a poem that I had written. In the cold silence of the viewing room, I sang him the song I had always promised him I would play. I then placed my guitar pick and the poem in the casket with him. I imagined that my grandfather was in heaven, listening to me finally singing him that song. At least I had kept my promise, albeit much too late.

The tragedy is that I didn't learn the lesson not to take life for granted until he passed away. I had been given an opportunity to make up for the time I lost with my grandmother, but instead of seizing it, I squandered it. Sadly, there are some decisions in life that we just can't take back.

Life always moves on, with or without us, and so my life has also moved on from my grandfather's death. Yet in the cycle of life we know that, despite death, new life comes and with it, new opportunities and second chances. I learned my lesson the hard way when I lost my grandfather and I refuse to make the same mistake again. Life is precious and it is short. Life is a gift from God. Each day is a new opportunity to express to those we cherish that we love them. Each day is a new opportunity to live the life that God called and created us to live, all for His glory. Let's not squander these beautiful opportunities.

I don't regret the lesson I learned; in fact, I cherish it. Some people go their entire lives and never realize the truth until it is too late. I just regret that I didn't learn it sooner and under different circumstances.

It's funny, all my childhood I thought there was nothing I could relate to my grandparents about; yet, in their death they both taught me one of the greatest lessons of all.

"Lord, make me to know my end, and what is the measure of my days, that I may know how frail I am. Indeed, You have made my days as handbreadths, and my age is nothing before You; certainly every man at his best state is but vapor. Surely every man walks about like a shadow; surely they busy themselves in vain; he heaps up riches, and does not know who will gather them. And now, Lord, what do I wait for? My hope is in You."

Psalm 39:4-7

A Friend's Sonnet

Why did you leave me when I needed you?
Why did you say you had to go away?
In your rash decision what could I do?
What could I do when you chose not to stay?

Many lonely months have long since passed by.
Yet the pain of friendship lost is still there.
My memory is nothing but a sad sigh.
My dear friend, where are you; do you not care?

As I look back at life, now I can see
That the day you left was a day of pain.
I won't forget you; please don't forget me.
For I know that one day we'll meet again.

Your love in my life has never parted.
In quiet hope I wait. Brokenhearted.

This poem was written for a dear friend of mine, a very godly man, who followed his calling to another state to serve the Lord in ministry. At the time, I was a senior in high school and I still lacked the maturity to understand the reasons for his decision.

You see, this man was my youth pastor at a time in my life when I was just beginning to really develop an awareness for the deeper things of God. For many years of my childhood I had labored under the misconception that being a Christian was about a place, a label, a tradition. It was in high school that I had my own "road to Damascus" experience and I began to learn that being a Christian is about having a personal relationship with Jesus Christ.

God blessed me with many godly friends who not only demonstrated to me a level of commitment to God that I later realized even many adults lack, but they also stood by my side to challenge me to dig deeper and to go further in my own walk, and it was our youth pastor, Jeff, who led the way.

When he moved away I felt saddened, betrayed, and forgotten, though in hindsight I know he made the right decision. When I had to write a sonnet for my high school English class, I made Jeff's departure the subject of my poem because those emotions were still raw for me.

Several years later, in the mountains of Idyllwild, I had an experience where the Lord really spoke to me concerning the subject of people in our lives leaving us. It was a moment at the end of summer camp, as all the staff (which I was a part) were about to go home.

The staff that worked at Idyllwild Pines camp the summer of 1994 was truly an anointed group of individuals. We all bonded the first weekend we were together and for the next two months we served, played, worshiped, rejoiced, and wept together. It was a group brought together "for such a time as this" in the very biblical sense. The problem was that we were all from different parts of California, so as the summer began to draw to a close the impending goodbyes began to weigh heavily on my heart.

I was walking by myself in the forest one night, lamenting to the Lord about all the people in my life that had left me up to that point. In one of those moments where you can feel the presence of the Holy Spirit so thick, I audibly heard Him draw my attention to the stars in the night sky. "Erik, see each one of those stars? Each one is a goodbye that you are *going* to make in this life." I was in such shock, and of course this wasn't the reassurance I had been hoping to hear, that I literally burst into tears.

Suddenly, a ball of fire shot across the sky from behind me and totally enveloped the night sky in a blinding light. In an instant, all the stars were gone. Needless to say, I was stunned silent as I watched the light slowly fade and the warm darkness of the summer night returned.

My feet were glued to the ground, my face still staring up to the sky, when I heard footsteps and laughter coming up the trail toward me. The sound broke my daze and I looked down to see two of my closest friends that summer, Justin and Jeremy, coming up the trail. They were jostling each other and having a great time, seemingly oblivious to what had just taken place.

I remember saying, "Did you guys see *that?*" I must have been an odd sight with tears streaming down my face and eyes wide in amazement! They both replied with a confused, "See what?" I carefully described what had just taken place. Neither of them knew what I was talking about and both of them probably thought I was crazy. I could see in their eyes that they were being honest with me.

As they walked away, I was bewildered that they hadn't seen what I saw. After all, the light was so bright that people had to have seen it for miles.

Then understanding hit me like a bolt of lightning! Have you ever presumptuously reacted to something a person said *before* they had actually finished their thought? That's what I had mistakenly done. You see, God was most certainly preparing me for goodbyes as numerous as the stars in the mountain sky, but He was also reminding me that His presence in my life would never fade. All goodbyes would become invisible next to His faithfulness. As I was filled with an overwhelming sense of peace and of being loved, my sorrow immediately turned to joy.

God had gently, yet dramatically, reminded me that though people may come and go from our lives, He will never leave our side. He will never forsake or abandon us and He never gets bored of us or emotionally distances

Himself. He is constant. He is the very definition of the word "faithful."

I had a second realization after the first one. God knows who I am! I know that sounds like a no-brainer, but seriously, think about it. Haven't you at one point or another felt like just a face in the crowd? There are billions of people alive on the planet and Jesus died for each one of them. He hears all of them. Don't you ever wonder if your voice gets drowned out in the roar? Let me assure you, God most definitely sees your individual face in the crowd and He is most certainly involved in the affairs of your life.

In fact, God wants you to have the deepest, most personal and intimate relationship you can imagine with Him. Think about it. He is with you at all times and He knows you better than you know yourself. Talk about intimacy!

Ever had a private joke between you and a best friend? You can be in a group when someone says some random word, then you and your best friend bust up laughing and no one else in the group understands what is so funny. It's a memory just between the two of you. That's why Justin and Jeremy had no idea what I was talking about that night in Idyllwild. What had taken place was meant just for me.

If you are struggling with the revolving door of human relationships or if you are just unsure of where you stand with God, let me assure you that God knows everything about you, the good and the bad, and He loves you anyway. He loves you with such a deep abiding passion that He died on a cross so that the barrier of sin could be removed and you could spend eternity in fellowship with Him. God will never leave you or abandon you. He will be your best friend, if you would only receive what He is offering.

"There is a friend who sticks closer than a brother."
Proverbs 18:24

"Greater love has no one than this, than to lay down one's life for his friends. You are My friends if you do whatever I command you."
John 15:13-14

The Dreamer

In what shadow does uncertainty crowd.
Beyond the unknown of life's earthly shroud?

Within those souls where callous hearts tend.
Such sadness of heart, yet true love can mend.

In what freedom can bondage be blamed?
When prisoner and jailer are one and the same?

Yet in a dreamer's heart exists the hope of a slave not free.
Something the world's finite reality is too blind to see.

Not only what exists but even hope to come.
True freedom may exist in the dreams of some.

No person can forget dreams such as these.
That cynics don't, but dreamers see.

I've always been a dreamer. When I was a young child in elementary school I remember signing my science homework under the name, "Dr. Erik Sahakian." Years later, when I was writing movie scripts in junior high, I had a name placard on my desk that said, "Erik Sahakian: Movie Producer." In hindsight, I certainly needed a big dose of humility, but at the time I was pretty serious about those designations.

A dreamer is someone who has vision and is willing to step out in faith and trust God. Sometimes the dreamer has the opportunity to witness the fruit of the vision and sometimes they are called to plant the seeds of the vision for someone else to harvest. First Corinthians 3:7 says, "So then neither he who plants is anything, nor he who waters, but God who gives the increase."

It's all for God's glory that we should be obedient to follow through on the vision He imparts to us. The end result is His responsibility. Our responsibility is to be faithfully obedient, as it says in First Samuel 15:22, "to obey is better than sacrifice."

This doesn't mean that everything will turn out the way we expect. Often God calls us to do a work that plays out much differently than our own expectations, but don't ever let that discourage you. Remember, He is our Lord and our vision needs to always be aligned with and in submission to His vision. Jesus said in Matthew 6:33, "But seek first the kingdom of God and His righteousness, and all these things shall be added to you."

God created you for a specific purpose and there is a vision He wants to impart to you. All you need to do is be open to receive and willing to follow.

"My sheep hear My voice, and I know them, and they follow Me."

John 10:27

"Most assuredly, I say to you, he who believes in Me, the works that I do he will do also; and greater works than these he will do, because I go to My Father."

John 14:12

Life Without You

The days pass on in piercing loneliness.
Like a summer night sky that no stars possess.
These thoughts fill my soul with a hollow confusion.
They invade my dreams and call them illusions.

As the seasons pass and dark days go by
Torrents of tears flow as I cry.
For a life without You is a life such as this
To live in despair without Your embrace.

Come take my life for I need You so.
Only Your forgiveness could erase my woe.
Your love, so sweet, dries away my tears
And having You near me calms my dark fears.

A life without You is a life of death.
For in Your love, I draw my life's breath.

Have you ever noticed that when you are in sin you don't feel close to God? Some people try to put the blame on God, as if He was the one who abandoned the relationship. I once saw a drawing that illustrated this truth very well. It showed a guy resting on his luggage in the middle of a desert and it said, "If you haven't felt God lately, guess who moved?"

The truth is that it isn't God who abandons us—it's we who abandon Him. Whenever we choose to follow after the desires of our flesh, worldly ambitions, and sinful behavior, we effectively walk away from our first love.

I remember this one time I was in a store with Maksim when he was around three years old. He was holding my hand, but then he saw a toy that captured his attention, so he willfully let go of me and ran to get a closer look. I was carefully watching him the entire time. When he was satisfied he looked around, didn't see me right away, and started to panic. In that moment, Maksim perceived that he was lost because he thought he had been separated from me. We often do that to God. We let go of His hand to dabble in sin, then we become confused when we feel lost and separated from Him.

David said it best in Psalm 51:4 when he wrote, "Against You, You only, have I sinned, and done this evil in Your sight." When you truly love someone you won't intentionally go out of your way to hurt them, especially when you already know what would be hurtful to them.

God hates sin and because He loves us it hurts Him to see us sin.

If we claim to love Him, then we should be avoiding sin at all costs, not just for our own benefit, but also because we love Him. Of course, due to our own wretchedness, we still sin all the time and that should bother us as it did David. There is something seriously wrong when a person claims to love God, but has no remorse over their sinful behavior or any desire to change. Instead, when we sin, we should be driven to our knees asking for His forgiveness and supernatural strength to be victorious over our own sinful tendencies. A person who embraces a lifestyle of sin will not be able to have true fellowship with God.

Sin not only harms us and hurts God, but it also has a negative impact on our relationship with God. When we sin, we need to be quick to surrender that sin to Jesus!

"If we confess our sins, He is faithful and just to forgive us our sins and to cleanse us from all unrighteousness."

1 John 1:9

The Dying Prayer of General Armistead

What has become of this world
Once filled with innocent beauty?
A world where friends vow to be so forever
A country once framed on patriotic unity?

What disease could be so strong
As to turn brother against brother?
Neither you nor I could ever have known
That we'd be forced to betray one another.

The disease is war, the ravager of life
The fiery red horseman of death.
It swallows the hope of the nation.
It lives on our last dying breath.

The bloody screams of terror still ring in my ear
My eyes are aflame with fire.
Where is the victory in this world of hate?
Where is the truth? Who is the liar?

For in gentle meadows where friends once sat
The golden fields are now stained red.
Yet through the din and the smoke filled sky, I search.
My brother where are you? Please don't be dead!

Just one last time I need to see you
For I know our friendship is stronger than war.

Dear God, allow me this one last prayer
To see my dear friend, General Hancock, once more.

Suddenly I feel a sharp tearing sting
As I hear voices screaming my name.
Then I notice my hands now covered in blood
And I fall in excruciating pain.

Though war may destroy the body I have
There is one thing war shall not do.
It can never destroy the love of a friend
Nor erase my memory of you.

As my eyes slowly close and the sounds fade away
I weep at this tragic end.
Yet into a world of peace, without sorrow I go.
Till we meet again, God keep you my friend.

It wasn't until I was in college that I began to really develop an interest and appreciation for history, especially American History. Like most children, when I was younger I thought history was the most boring subject in the world. However, in college I caught the history bug and it has stayed with me ever since.

One event in our nation's history that has always fascinated me was the three-day Battle of Gettysburg, which was a major turning point in the Civil War in 1863.

Back in 2007, I had the opportunity to visit the battleground in Gettysburg, Pennsylvania. The fields were so lush and green with blue skies and fluffy clouds above. It was difficult to imagine that there was a time when the ground there was soaked red with blood. In that one battle alone, there were approximately fifty-thousand casualties.

The Civil War was a profound, important, and yet tragic event because so many lives, families, and friendships were torn apart. It is ironic that the bloodiest war in our nation's history was perpetrated by none other than ourselves. I used to have a sculpture that sat on the corner of my desk in my office. It showed two American bald eagles, one holding the Union flag and the other holding the Confederate flag, coming at each other with talons raised. That was the Civil War.

In studying the history of the Civil War, I became aware of two men, dear friends, who had fought alongside each other as officers in the United Stated Army. When the Civil War broke out, both felt drawn to opposite sides. Lewis

Addison Armistead went to the Confederate side and Winfield Scott Hancock remained with the Union. It is said that Armistead's last words to his friend, Hancock, at a farewell party the night before he departed to the Confederate Army were, "Goodbye, you can never know what this has cost me." They would never see each other alive again.

Several years later, during the Battle of Gettysburg, both were informed that the other was physically present and both, unbeknownst to one another, had hoped to reunite after the battle was over. This never happened as Brigadier General Armistead and Major General Hancock were both wounded during the course of the battle. Armistead would die, but Hancock survived.

These two men, who were physically separated by war, had a friendship and a love for one another that war was not able to separate. I was touched by their story and upon hearing it, wrote this poem in less than five minutes with tears streaming down my face. Why did this story impact me so much? I was inspired because it speaks of the bonds of friendship and love. It reminded me how special friends are and what a gift friendship truly is, especially when God is the foundation.

Proverbs 27:17 states, "As iron sharpens iron, so a man sharpens the countenance of his friend." That is such a beautiful picture of a godly friendship—two separate individuals, coming together and through their interaction with one another, improving and making each other better. That is the type of friendship that honors and pleases God.

It was this exact type of friendship that David and Jonathan shared. It says in First Samuel 18:1 that "the soul of Jonathan was knit to the soul of David, and Jonathan loved him as his own soul." In verse 3, the Bible emphasizes this point by going on to say, "Then Jonathan and David made a covenant, because he loved him as his own soul." True friendship, based on God, is a beautiful thing that the world often tries to imitate, but can never fully achieve.

The story of Generals Armistead and Hancock also reminded me that though friends often come and go, we have a friend, the truest and most loyal friend of all, Jesus, who will never leave or forsake us. Proverbs 18:24 tells us that "there is a friend who sticks closer than a brother." That friend is Jesus Christ and He loves us more than any human friend possibly could. In fact, Jesus said in John 15:13, "Greater love has no one than this, than to lay down one's life for his friends." And that's exactly what He did.

"A friend loves at all times"

Proverbs 17:17

A Child's Prayer

Reach out Your arms to hold me.
Draw me closer to Your heart.
With Your loving hands, wash away my tears.
May we never be apart.

Pour Your grace and peace upon me.
Please sustain me with Your love.
Through the storms and misty haze
I can still see the Son above.

Anchor me and hold me still
When I want to run and hide.
Calm me, like a frightened child.
Show me where true love abides.

The world may laugh and taunt me.
My dreams may come crashing down.
You will shelter me from the storm.
You will never let me down.

Jesus said in Matthew 18:3-4, "Assuredly, I say to you, unless you are converted and become as little children, you will by no means enter the kingdom of heaven. Therefore whoever humbles himself as this little child is the greatest in the kingdom of heaven."

When I think of a little child, two words automatically come to my mind: faith and humility.

Years ago, when Maksim was around two years old, we were at an outdoor church event. Towards the end of the day I picked up Maksim and started throwing him into the air and catching him as he came back down. Despite Juanita's nervous glances, I knew that everything was fine; besides, Maksim was having the time of his life and was laughing hysterically! Then I had a sudden realization—the possibility of me dropping him had not even crossed Maksim's mind. His faith in me was so secure that my failure to catch him was not even a remote possibility, and because of his faith in me, he was able to enter into a place of utter joy. That is the faith of a little child.

I have always admired childlike faith and I believe it is this kind of faith that Jesus is telling us that we must have if we are to receive eternal life. He is telling us to humble ourselves and become like little children who have utter devotion and faith in their heavenly Father.

We need to let go of our pride and the deception that we have the ability to save ourselves or that we can somehow earn our way into heaven through good works. We need to release what we think we know based on our education or experiences and accept with joy what He says is true in His Word. We need to abandon our dependence and trust in possessions, money, power, influence, prestige, talents, abilities, and any other idols we may have, and instead, seek Him as a child desperately seeks a parent for all their provision, nurturing, and security.

A little child's world is very small and their universe literally revolves around their parents. Do you remember how your earliest heroes were your mom and dad? We were all totally dependent on them and sought them out, not just to meet our basic needs, but for comfort, companionship, and protection as well. I remember being a little child and whenever I woke up from a bad dream, I bolted straight to my parents' bed. Or remember falling and scraping your knee? It was to your parents that you cried out for assistance! That is the humility of a child.

But then over time the influence of the world began to creep in and before we were even old enough to drive, we already thought we knew more than our parents did and hardly even wanted to be seen in public with them. What a tragedy! This very attitude crosses over into adulthood and is the very attitude of pride that leads so many to reject Jesus Christ!

The world and its shallow provisions and empty promises will fail us time and time again. People will fail us. We will even fail ourselves! Yet there is one who will never fail us. He offers us the free gift of eternal salvation based on grace. He died for us to save us because we are incapable of saving ourselves. He is the perfect Father, who will protect you, provide for you, and will never fail you. All you have to do is humble yourself with the faith of a little child and receive the gift of salvation through Jesus Christ.

Then, just like my son, Maksim, who was able to enter into a place of such peace and joy because of his faith in me, you can enter into a place of peace and joy beyond anything you could ever comprehend or imagine, if you put your faith in Jesus.

It can be a frightening prospect to a naturally prideful person to humble themselves and enter into a childlike faith. Please believe me when I say it is the most freeing experience in the world to just let go and trust Him to guide your life.

"Let the little children come to Me, and do not forbid them; for of such is the kingdom of God. Assuredly, I say to you, whoever does not receive the kingdom of God as a little child will by no means enter it."

Luke 18:16-17

Ending with the Beginning

I thought it might be interesting to end where it all began. You see, I first became a Christian at a Billy Graham crusade when I was around ten years old, but it wasn't until the spring of 1990, during my freshman year of high school, that I seriously committed my life to following Jesus Christ.

The year that followed was one marked by profound changes and miracles in my life. At the time, I was being mentored by a friend who fortunately had the foresight to challenge me to keep a journal of that year to document all that the Lord was doing in my life. What a priceless gift because I still have that journal to this day! What follows is my very first journal entry. I still get emotional when I read it. It is a testimony to the power of Jesus to transform a life that some had written off—even myself. I hope it is meaningful to you as well.

April 27, 1991

Memories can be such beautiful things. They can fill you with joy or sadness. They can bring back hurt or even someone special in your life. They can cause you to laugh or cry. Some seem almost too fantastic to have been real and others are just locked away. Tonight, God showed me His gracious love as I reflected on the memories of the past.

It was around this time, exactly one year ago, that God started to show me just how very real He was and how much He loved me. I was making true friends for the first time and people were willing to help me, especially Boaz. I had some serious issues—I was lonely, depressed, and friendless. I saw a bleak future and I felt no reason to continue living. But it was after seven years (God's number of completion) that God pulled me out of my pit of despair, when I finally surrendered to Him.

Around that same time, I remember one night in particular. My bedroom window was open and a cool summer breeze was blowing in. Outside, the stars sparkled like diamonds in the sky as the shadows of the trees danced back and forth on my wall. I had no idea what incredible healing God was about to do in me over the next few months. I remember listening to a recording of my friend, Mike, singing worship songs, and just reflecting. I wondered why all these great things were suddenly happening to me. For the first time in a long time I looked toward the future with a hopeful anticipation. Little did I realize that things were going to get even better.

That was a year ago and tonight, it was like reliving that memory. Once again, I was in my room listening to a recording of Mike singing. As I looked out the window it dawned on me that everything felt the same—the weather, the time of year, the scenery…everything. It was a perfect moment of déjà vu. Yet oddly something *was* different. I began to wonder what it was.

In the quiet of the night the Holy Spirit began to speak to me—*I* was different.

I was no longer the lonely, depressed kid with no friends. I realized that God had changed my life so completely that I didn't even recognize myself from the year before. It was as if I was looking into the life of another person. I suppose that is exactly what I was doing.

God had performed miracles in my life! He had healed old wounds that I never thought would go away. He had taken away the bitterness and replaced it with love.

I began to realize that in those years that I was trapped in the pit of despair, when I truly thought that God had abandoned me, He was actually the closest, holding me up when no one else was around.

I will never forget what God has done in my life and I will proclaim it loudly until the day I die. I will always cherish the day I finally came home and He welcomed me with tears and open arms.

"Therefore, if anyone is in Christ, he is a new creation; old things have passed away; behold, all things have become new."

2 Corinthians 5:17

Final Thoughts

Hopefully you have sensed a common theme throughout this book and that would be that Jesus Christ has utterly, profoundly, and permanently changed my life. Please believe me when I say the experiences and insights I have shared with you were not meant to draw attention to me. Paul said in Galatians 6:14, "God forbid that I should boast except in the cross of our Lord Jesus Christ." It is for God's glory and honor alone.

If you are already a faithful follower of Jesus Christ, my prayer is that this testimony has both encouraged and inspired you to press on even deeper in your relationship with Him. As the author of Hebrews 10:24 admonishes, "let us consider one another in order to stir up love and good works." For my brothers and sisters in Christ out there, I hope you have been stirred up!

Perhaps you are a Christian, but your walk has become stale and you find yourself in a place where it just seems you are going through the motions, or perhaps you have "left your first love," as described in Revelation 2:4, and are now living as a prodigal. These are both extremely dangerous places to be.

You may be wondering, *"How did I end up here?"* or *"Where did the joy go?"* Let me assure you that regardless of how you ended up in this place, God still loves you and wants you to experience "life more abundantly," as Jesus described in John 10:10.

So where did the detour occur? There is a strong likelihood that there is unresolved sin in your life and it has negatively impacted your relationship with Jesus Christ.

When David repented of his sin with Bathsheba (2 Samuel 11-12:13), he wrote in Psalm 51:4 and 12, "Against You, You only, have I sinned, and done this evil in Your sight. Restore to me the joy of Your salvation." In David's sin the joy of his salvation had been eroded. That is the danger of unresolved sin in our lives—it will zap our joy and make our walk with the Lord seem hollow and fruitless.

A second likelihood is that there is open disobedience to God's will for your life, which will also lead you down a path of fruitlessness. In First Samuel 15:22 we're told "to obey is better than sacrifice." Disobedience will lead you into rebellion and apathy, which will always lead you away from God.

Paul states in Ephesians 2:10, "For we are his workmanship, created in Christ Jesus for good works, which God prepared beforehand that we should walk in them." Walking the path which the Lord has for you will bring joy; refusing to walk the path will lead to sorrow. When God told Jonah to go to Nineveh (Jonah 1), he found out firsthand how miserable it can be when you disobey God's calling on your life (Jonah 2). Trust me, I know. This is what led me to the shadowlands.

If this describes you, follow David and Jonah's examples of confessing your sin to God and repenting of your behavior. Sin, disobedience, rebellion—all of these create a blockade in the river that is our walk with Jesus. Confess, repent, and watch that blockade disappear and the water of life will flow freely once again!

Of course, there is another possibility—perhaps you have never genuinely accepted Jesus Christ as your savior.

Which brings me to my final point. If you do not have a personal relationship with Jesus Christ, I hope and pray this book has encouraged you to make one. If this describes where you are in life right now, hopefully you are now wondering what to do next.

First, you need to know the gospel ("good news") concerning Jesus Christ. First Corinthians 15:1-4 states, "Moreover, brethren, I declare to you the gospel which I preached to you, which also you received and in which you stand, by which also you are saved, if you hold fast that word which I preached to you—unless you believed in vain. For I delivered to you first of all that which I also received: that Christ died for our sins according to the Scriptures, and that He was buried, and that He rose again the third day according to the Scriptures."

Second, you must confess and believe you are a sinner and that Christ died for your sins and resurrected from the grave. It is promised in First John 1:9 that "If we confess our sins, He is faithful and just to forgive us our sins and to cleanse us from all unrighteousness." Romans 10:9-10 declares "that if you confess with your mouth the Lord Jesus and believe in your heart that God has raised Him from the dead, you will be saved. For with the heart one believes unto righteousness, and with the mouth confession is made unto salvation."

Finally, you need to understand that salvation is a free gift which none of us could ever earn based on our flawed attempt to work our way into heaven. Ephesians 2:8-9 says, "For by grace you have been saved through faith, and that not of yourselves; it is the gift of God, not of works, lest anyone should boast." Grace is unmerited favor and it carries the idea of receiving something we *don't* deserve. That is why salvation is a gift—you just need to receive it.

Once you have accepted Christ as Lord of your life, you now have the assurance of eternal life. First John 5:11-13 proclaims, "And this is the testimony: that God has given us eternal life, and this life is in His Son. He who has the Son has life; he who does not have the Son of God does not have life. These things I have written to you who believe in the name of the Son of God, that you may know that you have eternal life, and that you may continue to believe in the name of the Son of God."

So what will you do? The time is now. Paul wrote in Second Corinthians 6:2, "Behold, now is the accepted time; behold, now is the day of salvation." Don't put it off a moment longer. Every step of your life has purposefully brought you to this final page. It's time to make a decision once and for all. Who is Jesus Christ to you? This is the most important question you will ever ask yourself because your answer to this question will determine your eternity. I am praying you choose wisely.

"Behold, I stand at the door and knock. If anyone hears My voice and opens the door, I will come in to him."

Revelation 3:20

"I have come that they may have life, and that they may have it more abundantly."

John 10:10

A Prayer of Repentance and Salvation

Simply make this prayer your own as you speak honestly from your heart to the God who loves you.

Lord Jesus, I confess to You that I am a sinner and I acknowledge that I am incapable of saving myself; therefore, I need You to save me.

I believe You are the one and only true God, and that You took the form of a man so that You could die on the cross and pay the penalty of sin in my place.

I believe You resurrected from the grave on the third day and in doing so, You broke the bondage of sin and opened the door for me to have eternal fellowship with You.

I repent of my sins and I accept the free gift of salvation that You extend to me.

I choose to live a life of victory and freedom from sin and condemnation through the blood and authority of Jesus Christ.

I am Yours, forever.

Moving Forward

If you are a new believer in Jesus, it is essential that you spend time reading the Bible, praying, and connecting with other believers at a local church. Like any other relationship, you will get out of it what you put into it. So you need to spend time with Jesus, getting to know Him. He already knows you, better than you know yourself, but you need to grow in your understanding and knowledge of Him and His plan for your life.

To do this you must spend time praying, which is very simple—you just "talk" to God. Nothing fancy. Just be real and be yourself. There are no special words or phrases you need to repeat; instead, just speak honestly with Him. Jeremiah 29:12-13 promises, "Then you will call upon Me and go and pray to Me, and I will listen to you. And you will seek Me and find Me, when you search for Me with all your heart."

You also need to get a Bible. The Bible is God's Word in written form. Think of it as an instruction manual and love letter, all wrapped into one package. If you want to learn about God and what it means to be a Christian, He has revealed all this in the Bible. The Bible is spiritual food for our souls; it's not optional if we want our souls to live and thrive. Jeremiah 15:16 proclaims, "Your words were found, and I ate them, and Your word was to me the joy and rejoicing of my heart; for I am called by Your name, O Lord God of hosts."

Finally, it is essential to get plugged into a solid Bible-teaching church. Life is hard and being a Christian is not easy. None of us are meant to go about it alone. In fact, when we are alone we are very vulnerable to spiritual attack. Within a group of other believers we have fellowship, encouragement, an eternal family, a place for help, accountability, love, people to pray for us, and so much more. Hebrews 10:24-25 says, "And let us consider one another in order to stir up love and good works, not forsaking the assembling of ourselves together, as is the manner of some, but exhorting one another."

God has a plan and purpose for our lives. Romans 12:4-5 reminds us, "For as we have many members in one body, but all the members do not have the same function, so we, being many, are one body in Christ, and individually members of one another." Just as the human body has many parts, but it is one body, you are now a key member with a specific role to fill in the body of Christ, which is His church.

Jesus said in Luke 15:10, "Likewise, I say to you, there is joy in the presence of the angels of God over one sinner who repents." There is joy in heaven right now as your lifelong journey with Jesus has just begun! I may not know you personally, but as I am writing these words I am thinking about you and praying for you.

Welcome to the Family!

About the Author

Erik V. Sahakian has committed his life to serving Jesus Christ through teaching God's inerrant Word, ministering to the body of Christ, and writing. He joyfully worships and serves with his wife and children at Wildwood Calvary Chapel in Yucaipa, CA.

Visit www.eriksahakian.com to learn more.

www.ingramcontent.com/pod-product-compliance
Lightning Source LLC
LaVergne TN
LVHW051525070426
835507LV00023B/3305